GRAMERCY GREAT MASTERS

Acknowledgments

The publishers would like to thank the museums for reproduction permission and in particular the **BRIDGEMAN ART LIBRARY** and **SCALA Istituto Fotografico Editoriale** for their help in supplying the illustrations for the book.

Accademia, Florence: Bearded Slave; The Young Slave; The Awakening Slave; The Slave (Atlas).
British Museum, London: Study for The Creation of Adam; Study for The Last Judgment.
Cappelle Medicee, Florence: The Tomb of Lorenzo de' Medici; The Tomb of Giuliano de' Medici.
Galleria dell'Accademia, Florence: David.
Louvre, Paris: The Dying Slave.
Museo del Bargello, Florence: Bacchus; Pitti Tondo.
Museo dell'Opera del Duomo, Florence: Pietà.
Notre Dame, Bruges: Bruges Madonna.
Palazzo degli Uffizi, Florence: The Holy Family (Doni Tondo).
Palazzo Vecchio, Florence: The Victory.
Royal Academy of Art, London: Taddei Tondo.
S. Pietro in Vincoli, Rome: The Tomb of Pope Julius II.
S. Maria sopra Minerva, Rome: The Risen Christ.
Basilica di S.Pietro, Rome: Pietà.
Vatican Museums, Rome: View of the vault before the last restoration; Deluge; The Fall and Expulsion (Sistine Chapel ceiling); The Creation of Eve (Sistine Chapel ceiling); The Creation of Adam (Sistine Chapel ceiling); View of the vault from God Separating Earth from Water; The Creation of the Sun, Moon and Stars (Sistine Chapel ceiling); Ignudi near God Separating Earth from Water and The Persian Sybil; Ignudo (Sistine Chapel ceiling); Delfic Sybil; Cuman Sybil; Libyan Sybil; Geremiah (Sistine Chapel ceiling); View of the vault after the last restoration; The Last Judgment (Sistine Chapel); Christ and the Virgin (The Last Judgment detail); Angels and Archangels (The Last Judgment detail); The Damned (The Last Judgment detail); St. Bartholomew (The Last Judgment detail); Crucifixion of St. Peter; The Last Judgment.

Published by Gramercy Books
distributed by Random House Value Publishing, Inc.
40 Engelhard Avenue
Avenel, New Jersey 07001

Printed and bound in Italy

ISBN: 0-517-12400-9

10 9 8 7 6 5 4 3 2 1

Michelangelo

GRAMERCY BOOKS

NEW YORK • AVENEL

11-20-97

11-20-97

Michelangelo
His Life and Works

Michelangelo Buonarroti was born at Caprese, a small hill town in Tuscany, on March 6, 1475. His father, Lodovico di Leonardo di Buonarroto Simoni, had been sent there as magistrate for six months. When his term of office ended, just a few weeks after Michelangelo was born, Lodovico took his family back to Settignano, a village just outside Florence. Here Michelangelo was cared for by a nurse who came from a family of stonemasons, and later in life he would claim that this was when he first discovered his interest in sculpture.

Michelangelo was the second of the five sons born to Francesca di Neri di Miniato del Serra before her death in 1481. His father remarried four years later, and the family moved to Florence, where they lived in a house near the Church of Santa Croce. Lodovico Buonarroti wanted his sons to enter the wool and silk trade, and Michelangelo was sent to study grammar and arithmetic with Francesco Galatea da Urbino. Despite his father's opposition, Michelangelo developed his talent for drawing, and on April 1, 1488, he was apprenticed for three years to the painter Domenico Ghirlandaio. Although Michelangelo later denied this apprenticeship, it is confirmed by several contemporary chroniclers. Michelangelo's earliest known drawings date from this period, and they are mainly copies of figures taken from frescoes done in Florence by Masaccio and Giotto.

Michelangelo left Ghirlandaio's workshop in 1489, before the end of his apprenticeship, and went to study the collection of antique sculptures belonging to the rich and powerful Medici family, who were the rulers of Florence at the time. Lorenzo the Magnificent, an enthusiastic patron of the arts, had turned his garden into an academy where young sculptors could copy the statues of the classical period under the guidance of Bertoldo di Giovanni, a former pupil of Donatello. Lorenzo gave Michelangelo a small stipend and introduced him to the

9

The Fall and Expulsion
(detail)

10

Medici court, where he met such leading figures of the Renaissance as the philosopher Marsilio Ficino, who did much to spread the ideas of Plato, and the poet Angelo Politian, who was also a professor of Greek and Latin at the University of Florence.

Two of Michelangelo's sculptures finished between 1490 and 1492 are *The Madonna of the Stairs* and *The Battle of the Centaurs*. In the first he used Donatello's technique of *rilievo stiacciato*, relief work in which the scene portrayed stands out only slightly from the marble slab on which it is carved, so that the effect is similar to a painting. The figure of the Madonna is seen in profile and takes up the whole length of the work. The Holy Child is being suckled, and on the stairs in the background a group of *putti*, or cherubs, holds a shroud. This is probably an allusion to the future sacrifice of Christ: the contrast between life and death was a recurring theme in Michelangelo's later art.

The subject of *The Battle of the Centaurs*, taken from classical mythology, was suggested to Michelangelo by Politian. The sculpture is based on the battle scenes carved on the Roman sarcophagi that Michelangelo had studied in the garden of Lorenzo the Magnificent, but it also extols the beauty of the male nude, recurrent in Michelangelo's work.

Lorenzo the Magnificent died in April 1492, and although his son and successor Piero de' Medici continued his patronage of young artists, Michelangelo received only one commission from him. This was for a statue to be built from the heavy snow that fell in Florence on January 20, 1494, clearly a short-lived work that was nevertheless greatly admired by the nobles of the city. Michelangelo had already returned to live in his father's house, and the success of the statue finally persuaded Lodovico that his errant son really had an outstanding talent. He was allowed to study anatomy with the prior of the Hospital of Santo Spirito, for whom he carved a wooden crucifix. Charles VIII of France invaded Italy in 1494, and in October, only a few days before the army reached Florence, Michelangelo fled the city. He traveled to Venice and then back down to Bologna, where he lived for a year in the home of Giovanni Francesco Aldrovandi, one of the leading nobles of the city. Michelangelo was able to see the sculptures of Jacopo della Quercia in the Basilica of San Petronio, and he carved three small statues, *St. Procolus*, *St. Petronius* and an *Angel*, for the Church of San Domenico.

THE FIRST PERIOD IN ROME (1496–1501)

In November 1494 a popular rebellion in Florence, led by the fanatical religious reformer Gerolamo Savonarola, overthrew Piero de' Medici and his family. Savonarola preached against Renaissance art but Michelangelo admired his commitment to democracy and honesty in public virtue. When he returned to Florence in November 1495 he stayed with Pierfrancesco de' Medici who, despite his name, was a sympathizer of the new republic. Michelangelo carved a small statue for him known as *The Young St. John*, but it has been lost. Another lifesize statue carved in the same year, called *The Sleeping Cupid*, has also been lost. Sculpted in the classical manner, it was even buried for a short time to give it a convincingly authentic finish. When the statue was sent to Rome, it was sold by an art merchant as a genuine antique to Cardinal Raffaele Riario, who on discovering the ruse was curious to meet this skillful imitator of classical sculptures and invited Michelangelo to Rome. Armed with a letter of presentation from Pierfrancesco de' Medici, Michelangelo set out from Florence in June 1496.

In Rome, Cardinal Riario commissioned a statue of *Bacchus* portrayed as a youth, which was bought by the banker Jacopo Galli. This was Michelangelo's first major work. Galli in turn obtained a commission for Michelangelo from the French cardinal Jean Villiers de la Groslaye for the *Pietà*, showing the dead Christ in the arms of His mother, which was completed in 1499 and placed in St. Peter's Basilica. This is the only sculpture that Michelangelo ever signed, and the art historian Giorgio Vasari, whose *Lives of the Most Eminent Painters, Sculptors and Architects* was published in 1550, wrote that this was because Michelangelo had overheard a group of visitors from Milan praising the statue, which they thought was by the Milanese artist Cristoforo Solari. According to Vasari, Michelangelo stole into St. Peter's at midnight with a lantern, and signed the sculpture of the Madonna on the sash across her breast. The detail and realism of this sculpture is marvelous, charging with emotion the beautifully sculpted bodies with their exquisite draperies in flawless white marble, and as Vasari comments, "It is certainly a miracle that a formless block of stone could ever have been reduced to a perfection that nature is scarcely able to create in the flesh."

RETURN TO FLORENCE (1501–1505)

The success of the *Pietà* brought Michelangelo fame as a sculptor, and in the spring of 1501 he was invited to return to Florence by the governors

Persian Sybil
(detail)

13

Zacariah
(detail)

14

of the Republic. In June he was commissioned by Cardinal Francesco Piccolomini, later Pope Pius III, to carve fifteen small statues for the altar of his family chapel in Siena Cathedral, but no sooner had he started work on this series than he received a far more prestigious commission. This came from an influential guild of Florentine merchants, with the approval of the city's chief magistrate, Pier Soderini, and the subject was to be *David*. The block of marble offered to Michelangelo for this work was some eighteen feet high and had already been in Florence for about forty years, ever since Agostino di Duccio had ruined it in his unsuccessful attempts to carve it. Michelangelo squared the stone off again before starting work, and the statue was erected in Florence's central Piazza della Signoria on September 8, 1504. The Florentines immediately acclaimed it as a symbol of their freedom and their struggle against tyranny.

This new triumph increased his fame and the number of commissions he received, creating an intolerably heavy workload. He was able to complete no more than two of the fifteen statues ordered by Cardinal Piccolomini, and two more had to be finished by his assistants. A bronze version of *David* was commissioned by the rulers of Florence, as a gift to Maréchal de Gié, a nobleman who at the time kept a tight hold on the reins of power in France, an ally of Florence. Michelangelo left Florence before the statue was finished, and it was completed in 1508 by Benedetto de Rovezzano.

It is not known exactly when Michelangelo worked on the sculpture of the Madonna and Child known as *The Bruges Madonna*. It was certainly completed by 1506, when it was sold by the artist to the Cathedral of Bruges in Belgium.

The *Taddei Tondo* and the *Pitti Tondo* are two circular relief sculptures in marble carved around 1505, and both show the Madonna and the Holy Child with the young St. John. The figures gradually emerge from the marble; they seem unfinished, but this was intentional as Michelangelo conceived his sculpture as the art of taking away only what was superfluous from the block of stone, rather than imposing a predetermined form on it. His task was to discover and bring to life the statue that was in the marble. Thus, it became increasingly unnecessary for him to arrive at the same fineness of surface texture that was striking in his *Pietà* in St. Peter's.

Given Michelangelo's views on this subject, it is difficult to decide whether the statue of *St. Matthew* now in the Accademia Gallery of Florence was left unfinished deliberately or not. The statue is the only one of a series of twelve intended to represent the Apostles that was ever started. Michelangelo received the commission from Florence Cathedral in 1503, but he made such slow progress on the project, probably because of his many other commitments, that the commission was canceled two years later. The figure of the saint does seem to be struggling to free himself from the marble, and perhaps this half-finished statue abandoned in Michelangelo's workshop inspired his later experiments.

Michelangelo had done little painting since he left his apprenticeship with Ghirlandaio, and it can be assumed that this was because of his strong preference for sculpture. He made an exception in 1504 when he painted a *Holy Family*, also known as the *Doni Tondo*, to celebrate the marriage of Agnolo Doni and Maddalena Strozzi. The subject of the painting probably refers to the new family formed by the marriage. The figures of the Madonna, St. Joseph and the Holy Child are arranged in a close group in the foreground, full of lively movement. Behind a low wall that sharply divides the space of the picture is the young St. John, and set against a desolate landscape in the background is a group of male nudes. It seems that the different parts of this painting were an allusion to the three main epochs of human history as interpreted by the dominant religious ideology of the time. The nudes represent the world before the Ten Commandments were given to Moses. St. John stands for the world of the Old Testament, and the New Testament and the Redemption are symbolized by the birth of Christ. Such a complex interpretation of what appears to be a straightforward painting of the Holy Family might now be considered as being rather extravagant, but symbolism was a common feature of religious painting in the Renaissance, based on the classical studies of the Humanist philosophers as well as on the official doctrines of the Church of Rome.

Leonardo da Vinci, Michelangelo's great rival and his senior by some twenty years, had returned to Florence in 1500, and in 1503 started work on an enormous fresco in the Council Chamber of the Palazzo Vecchio, showing *The Battle of Anghiari*, a famous Florentine victory. The following year, the chief magistrate of the city, Pier Soderini, invited Michelangelo to paint a fresco of another Florentine victory on the opposite wall of the council chamber, *The Battle of Cascina*. Neither of the two artists completed these frescoes. Leonardo painted only the central part of the scene, but as this was in a wax technique with which the artist was experimenting at the time, with disastrous results, he stopped work in 1505. Michelangelo only had time to prepare the cartoon for his painting, as in March of the same year he was urgently recalled to Rome by Pope Julius II, who was

Ezechiel
(detail)

anxious to have Michelangelo design a magnificent tomb for him. The cartoon was studied by every young painter in Florence for many years after, and it had a vast influence on the subsequent development of Italian art. Sadly, it was finally cut into smaller pieces that have been lost or destroyed, but several copies of these fragments have survived. The best of these copies is the one attributed to his friend Aristotile da Sangallo, which shows Michelangelo's genius in the drawing of male nudes: a group of Florentine soldiers is depicted hurriedly climbing out of the waters of the River Arno, where they had been bathing to escape from the heat of summer, and preparing themselves for battle with the approaching army of Pisa.

THE TOMB OF JULIUS II AND THE SISTINE CHAPEL (1505–1516)

When Michelangelo returned to Rome in March 1505, Julius II ordered him to start work on an enormous tomb that would be a suitable commemoration of the pope's grandeur. The tomb was to be built inside St. Peter's Basilica, which was redesigned by the architect Donato Bramante. Michelangelo's plans were completed by the end of May. The huge freestanding pyramid, with a base measuring about thirty-six feet by twenty-four feet, was to have three tiers of columns decorated with forty statues leading up to a statue of Julius at the summit. Inside this massive structure, a vault for the sarcophagus of the pope was planned, to be entered by a door at the rear.

Michelangelo was so eager to start work on this new commission that he spent the rest of the year in the quarries of Carrara, where he carefully selected the blocks of marble to be used for the tomb, paying for them himself, as he expected to be reimbursed by the pope. In the meantime, however, Julius had lost much of his initial enthusiasm, and overwhelmed by the debts incurred for the planned rebuilding of St. Peter's and for his renewed military campaign against Perugia and Bologna, he refused to see Michelangelo when the artist returned to Rome. In April 1506, Michelangelo, gravely offended by the pope's behavior, left the city and went back to Florence, where he continued his work on the sculpture of *St. Matthew* and on his cartoon for *The Battle of Cascina*. Julius sent several letters to Michelangelo ordering him to return to Rome, but received no answer. The pope then attempted to use his influence on the rulers of Florence, and Pier Soderini at last convinced Michelangelo to reconcile his differences with Julius. Michelangelo set out for Bologna in November 1506, where Julius had just successfully ended his siege of the city. To celebrate the victory, Michelangelo agreed to cast a huge bronze statue of Julius to be erected in front of the Basilica of San Petronio, in the main square of Bologna. Much against his will, he spent the next fifteen months in the city working day and night on this statue, which was completed in February 1508 only to be destroyed three years later when the Bentivoglio family regained control of the city.

Michelangelo left Bologna as soon as the statue was finished, and returned to Florence. He stayed there until a letter from Julius recalled him to Rome in May 1508, where he was to start painting the frescoes on the vault of the Sistine Chapel in the Vatican. Once more the artist's work on the tomb for Julius was interrupted, and he would later describe this unfinished project as "the tragedy of my life." Giorgio Vasari and Ascanio Condivi, who both wrote biographies of Michelangelo while he was still alive, suggest that the architect Bramante had a hand in this new commission, supposing that Michelangelo's supremacy as a sculptor and his lack of experience in painting would doom him to failure and loss of favor with the pope. Michelangelo himself was unhappy with the commission, and on the receipt for the first payment for the frescoes, he meticulously specified that he was a sculptor.

The projected frescoes were a daunting challenge to Michelangelo. More than three thousand square feet was to be painted with biblical scenes, prophets and other figures. Michelangelo worked on the frescoes by himself for over four years, rejecting all offers of assistance from friends and painters, claiming that they were insufficiently talented for such a grandiose venture.

Michelangelo painted columns and arches on the ceiling of the chapel to divide it into a series of separate panels. The central panels show nine scenes from the Book of Genesis, arranged in chronological order starting from the end of the vault over the altar. The first panel is *God Dividing Light from Darkness*, and the frescoes then narrate the rest of the Creation, finishing with *Noah After the Flood*. All these panels have a naked youth sitting in each corner and farther down the curve of the vault is a row of prophets and sybils. Above the altar is Jonah, whose three days in the whale were interpreted as being a prefiguration of the Resurrection. Beneath the prophets and sybils are the forty generations of the ancestors of Christ, taken from the Gospel of St. Matthew, and in the corners of the ceiling there are four scenes from the Old Testament.

Michelangelo started work on the frescoes in July 1508, using scaffolding that he had designed himself. The technique of fresco painting

David and Goliath
(detail)

20

had been known since Roman times, and during the Renaissance it was brought to perfection. First the designs were traced onto a sheet of cardboard, called a cartoon, and the main outlines were perforated. This cartoon was held against the freshly plastered surface to be painted, and it was dusted over with soot. Another thin layer of plaster was laid on the surface, and over this the cartoon was redrawn. When the paint was applied, there was a chemical reaction that bonded the colors to the plaster. Only the area that could be painted in a single day was plastered at any one time, and the remaining plaster was cut away when work was finished in the evening. Although Michelangelo had learned the fresco technique when he was apprenticed to Ghirlandaio, his lack of practical experience at first led to unsatisfactory results. Mold started to form on the freshly painted surface because the plaster was too thinly diluted with water, but this problem was overcome when the pope sent Giuliano da Sangallo to teach Michelangelo how to use the medium correctly. Michelangelo used cartoons for the central part of the ceiling, but farther down the sides of the fresco he often painted freehand, directly onto the plaster.

The scenes from the Book of Genesis were painted in reverse order, working towards the altar, probably so that it could still be used for religious services. Julius occasionally came to check the progress of the ceiling, climbing up on the scaffolding to confer with Michelangelo. The artist was not content, however, as many of his letters of this period show. In 1508 he wrote to his father: "I have been here one year already, and have not had anything from the pope yet, and nor do I ask it, because my work is not going as well as I think it deserves to." The year after, Michelangelo wrote again to his father: "I am not happy here, and my health is not good. The work is hard, there is nobody to guide me and I have no money." It was at this time that Michelangelo abandoned the fresco for a year, complaining that the pope was not giving him enough attention.

This was undoubtedly true, as, following an important French victory, Julius was back at the head of his army, busily occupying the Italian towns of Faenza, Rimini and Ravenna. Yet again Michelangelo wrote to his father: "He has gone away and left me without orders or instructions, so I have no money at all and neither do I know what I have to do." The topic of money was frequently mentioned in Michelangelo's letters to his family. In October 1509 he wrote to his brother Buonarroto: "Here I am, working hard and with great physical effort. I have no friends at all, and nor do I want them, and I have not even enough time to eat well. So do not bother me again [with requests for money] or I will lose my patience with you." Michelangelo sent his father a hundred ducats in January 1510, to buy a shop for "Buonarroto and the others," closing with these words: "I have no money. This money that I am sending has been wrenched from my heart, and I do not find it fair for you to ask for it."

Despite Michelangelo's difficulties with his patron Julius, the first part of the vault, consisting of six of the main panels and the surrounding decorations, was completed in August 1511, with the pope officiating at two masses in the chapel in honor of the occasion. With the scaffolding demolished it was finally possible to have an unobstructed view of the fresco, and Julius declared himself pleased with the results. Michelangelo was far from satisfied, however, and he made several changes, increasing the proportions of many of the figures and adopting a freer and more rapid style. In October of the same year, the pope authorized Michelangelo to continue with the remaining part of the ceiling, assuring him that this time there would be no problems with payment. The fresco was finished in October 1512, and it was immediately acclaimed as a masterpiece by the entire papal court.

Having completed this long and difficult task, Michelangelo returned to his work on Julius's tomb. The pope died in March 1513 before it was finished, and his heirs negotiated a new agreement with Michelangelo in May of the following year. The original project was scaled down drastically, and it was no longer to be freestanding but set beneath an arch against a wall. The forty statues were reduced to twenty-eight, and Michelangelo started work on only three of these while still in Rome, one of Moses and two of figures known as *Slaves* or *Prisoners*. The *Moses*, now the main figure on the tomb that was finished only in 1545, is reputed to be a likeness of Julius himself.

FLORENCE AND THE MEDICI FAMILY (1516–1534)

After the death of Julius II in 1513, Giovanni de' Medici, the son of Lorenzo the Magnificent, was elected pope and took the name of Leo X. Wishing to leave his mark on his native city of Florence, of which the Medici family had regained control the previous year, Leo turned his attention to the various unfinished projects of his father and grandfather, Cosimo de' Medici. In 1515 he invited the submission of plans for the completion of the façade that Brunelleschi had designed for the Basilica of San Lorenzo, a church long associated with the Medici family. Raphael, Giuliano da Sangallo, Andrea Sansovino and Jacopo

Detail of the ribbed vault
(Sistine Chapel)

23

Sansovino all took part in the contest, but it was Michelangelo's design that was finally chosen, thus qualifying him not only as a sculptor and a painter but also as an architect.

Michelangelo spent four years on this project, even visiting Carrara again to select the marble to be used in the construction, but the contract for the façade was canceled in March 1520 after the death of two of Leo's relatives — Giuliano, Duke of Nemours, and Lorenzo, Duke of Urbino — had seriously depleted the Medici family resources.

Michelangelo had earlier offered to design a tomb for the ashes of the great Italian poet Dante, if these could be brought back to Florence from Ravenna, but Leo X rejected this proposal and instead ordered Michelangelo to start work on a second funeral chapel for the Medici family, in the same Basilica of San Lorenzo. Leo X died at the end of 1521, and the proposed chapel was reduced in size, containing only the tombs of Giuliano and Lorenzo. These were completed many years later, in 1534, and are decorated with four reclining marble statues, *Dawn*, *Day*, *Dusk* and *Night*, symbolizing the swift passage of time that leads inexorably to death, another frequent theme in Michelangelo's art.

Following the brief reign of Pope Adrian VI, who took little interest in the arts, Leo X's cousin Giulio de' Medici became pope in 1523, with the title of Clement VII. Clement added to Michelangelo's considerable workload by commissioning him to build the Laurentian Library, destined to house the precious library of the Medici family. The library was to be erected next to the Basilica of San Lorenzo, and Michelangelo prepared plans for every part of it, including the interior, for which he designed everything from the ceilings and floors to the bookshelves, reading desks and benches.

Michelangelo's work on the Medici Tombs and the Laurentian Library was interrupted by the overthrow of the Medici family and the restoration of the Florentine Republic in May 1527. Despite his natural aversion for all political matters, Michelangelo was appointed one of the leaders of the militia of Florence in January 1529 and was put in charge of the city fortifications when it was threatened by the combined armies of Pope Clement VII and the King of Spain, Charles V. In September 1529 Michelangelo fled Florence and went first to Ferrara and then to Venice. In November he was officially declared a "rebel" by the Florentine Republic, but he returned to the city the following month, brought back by the sudden death of his brother Buonarroto.

The Republic fell in August 1530, and the Medici family was restored to power. Michelangelo was forced into hiding until he was pardoned by Pope Clement for abandoning the various commissions that had been entrusted to him, on condition that he must immediately return to work on the Medici Tombs. Michelangelo complied with this order, but was soon forced to interrupt his work once again, summoned to Rome for yet another commission. The Medici Tombs were abandoned as they were nearing completion, but the Laurentian Library was finished only in 1558, under the supervision of Michelangelo's assistants Giorgio Vasari and Bartolomeo Ammannati.

A FINAL RETURN TO ROME (1534–1564)

Michelangelo left Florence for Rome on September 23, 1534, called by Clement VII to paint a vast fresco of *The Last Judgment* on the altar wall of the Sistine Chapel, a project that had been agreed upon at a meeting between the pope and the artist in the previous year. Clement died on September 25, but his successor, Paul III, confirmed the commission soon after Michelangelo's arrival in Rome. Naturally, this meant that Michelangelo was yet again prevented from working on the tomb of Julius II, and the new pope issued a decree freeing him from all contractual obligations to the Della Rovere family, the heirs of Julius, while *The Last Judgment* was being painted.

The preparation of the wall for the fresco was completed by 1536. This involved the building of a brick lining against the wall, slanting slightly inwards to prevent dust from settling on the painted surface. An existing fresco by Perugino was destroyed in the process. Michelangelo was sixty-one when he started painting *The Last Judgment*, helped in minor tasks by Francesco Amadori, his servant since 1529. While the scaffolding was being moved lower down the wall in 1540, Michelangelo fell and seriously injured his leg, but he refused to allow this accident to halt his work, keeping it a closely guarded secret. The fresco was officially inaugurated by Paul III on October 31, 1541, and it caused as great a sensation as had his previous work on the ceiling, although it is very different in character.

The Last Judgment is an immense scene of some four hundred figures grouped around Christ, who is judging mankind on the Last Day. By His side is the Virgin Mary, to whom the Sistine Chapel is dedicated, and many of the other figures in the upper part of the painting portray saints or prophets. The figure of Christ provides the

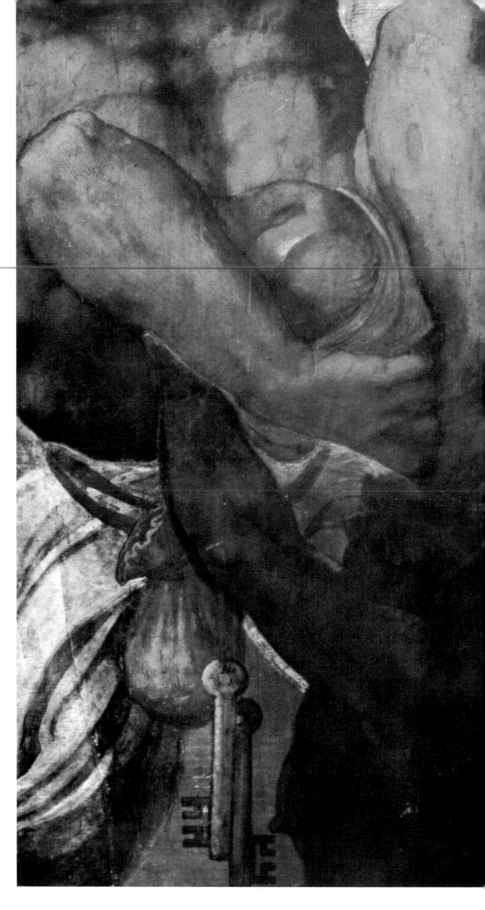

The Last Judgment
(detail)

26

key to the interpretation of the fresco. With His raised right arm He beckons the persons judged worthy of salvation upwards towards Heaven, while His left arm motions downwards to represent the descent of the damned to Hell. In the bottom left, the dead are rising from their tombs, summoned by the seven trumpets of a flight of angels. At the bottom, on the right, subjects from classical mythology are introduced. A crowd of sinners, ferried across the Styx by Charon, are being driven before Minos, one of the three judges of the Underworld, seen in the corner. This mingling of Christian and pagan themes is quite usual in the Renaissance, and here Michelangelo was inspired by the poetry of Dante. At the bottom of the fresco, in the center, is a gaping hole, generally interpreted as being the mouth of Hell. As it is just above the chapel altar during services it forms the backdrop for the cross, which represents Christ's offer of salvation for humanity. Semicircles at the top of the picture illustrate the symbols of Christ's suffering — the scourging post, the crown of thorns and the cross, carried by angels.

Despite its masterful depiction of movement, *The Last Judgment* is a gloomy and despondent work, strongly in contrast to the optimism of the frescoes painted thirty years earlier on the ceiling. Although this quality is obviously dictated by the subject portrayed, the end of the world as opposed to its creation, it also reflects Michelangelo's growing apprehension for his own destiny. In a poem that the artist wrote some ten years later, one of the many that he composed in his lifetime, he lamented that he was living merely "in the hostel of death." Although he lived to be almost ninety, Michelangelo was perpetually plagued by a sense of his impending doom, and he feared that on the Last Day he would be found unworthy of salvation. On the lower right-hand side of Christ is the bearded St. Bartholomew, who was martyred by being skinned alive. He is holding a pelt on which there is a reputed self-portrait of the artist. Christ's stern gaze of rebuke seems to be directed at Michelangelo himself.

Another aspect of the fresco that caused consternation was its enormous number of male nudes, deemed inappropriate for the chapel where services were often led by the pope himself. In 1564, shortly before Michelangelo's death, the Council of Trent, set up by Pope Paul III to counter the threat of the Protestant Reformation, gave orders to use painted loincloths to cover any part of the fresco judged to be obscene. The artist appointed for this task was one of Michelangelo's friends, the painter and sculptor Daniele da Volterra, who thus acquired the nickname of "Il Braghettone" — "The Breeches Maker."

An official cleaner for the frescoes in the Sistine Chapel was appointed as early as 1543, a job that was made necessary by the accumulation of soot from the candles used to light the chapel. Various repairs and alterations have been made to the fresco over the centuries, often with deplorable results, and in 1980 an ambitious project of restoration was started. This project, led by Carlo Pietrangeli, director of the Vatican Museums, with the collaboration of leading art experts and institutes from all over the world, was terminated in April 1994. Many of the overpainted loincloths were eliminated, and the colors of the fresco were returned to their original brilliance. While reactions to this restoration have been generally enthusiastic, some critics claim that, along with the grime of centuries, it has also removed many details that Michelangelo had repainted after the fresco had been finished.

The controversy aroused by the allegedly blasphemous obscenity of some of the figures of *The Last Judgment* when it was unveiled had little effect on Pope Paul III, who immediately commissioned Michelangelo to paint two frescoes for the Paoline Chapel in the Vatican, which had been consecrated by the pope himself in 1540. However, Michelangelo was still under contract to the heirs of Pope Julius II for the completion of the tomb that had been commissioned almost forty years earlier. At the insistence of Pope Paul III, a final contract for the tomb was signed in August 1542. It was to be relocated in a chapel of the Church of San Pietro in Vincoli, in Rome, where it still stands today. The forty statues originally planned and then reduced by a long series of contracts were replaced by a group of only three statues. One of these was to be the *Moses* on which Michelangelo had been working intermittently since 1515. The other two statues, *Leah* and *Rachel*, were carved by Raffaello da Montelupo, and the tomb was finally completed in February 1545.

Freedom from this commitment that had oppressed him for so many years meant that in November 1542 Michelangelo could start work on the first of the two frescoes in the Paoline Chapel, *The Conversion of St. Paul.* In July and August of 1544 the artist fell seriously ill, perhaps as a result of the sheer physical exhaustion caused by years of almost ceaseless activity on frescoes, climbing up and down the scaffolding and working in extremely uncomfortable positions, and he had to be cared for in the home of his friend Luigi del Riccio. Despite this interruption, *The Conversion of St. Paul* was finished in 1545, and Michelangelo promptly started work on the other fresco, showing *The Crucifixion of St. Peter*, which was completed in 1550. At this time he was almost seventy-five years old, and as he confided to another friend, Giorgio Vasari, "After a certain age, painting, and particularly the painting of frescoes, is no job for an old man." For the rest of his life, Michelangelo concentrated on sculpture and architecture.

In 1537, Michelangelo had already been commissioned by Pope Paul III to redesign the square in front of the Capitol in Rome to provide a suitable setting for the ancient Roman statue of Marcus Aurelius on horseback that the pope intended to erect there as a symbol of government and justice. Michelangelo designed a large oval for the main part of the square, the first time that this shape was used in Renaissance architecture, and he placed the statue of Marcus Aurelius at the center of this oval. He planned new façades for the two palaces flanking the square, but like most of his architectural projects, neither of these was finished before his death.

After Antonio da Sangallo, the chief architect of St. Peter's Basilica, died in 1546, Pope Paul III appointed Michelangelo in his place. Building had been going on at St. Peter's since 1505, and Michelangelo was faced with the problem of continuing a project that had been worked on previously by two other architects, Bramante and Raphael, as well as by Sangallo. He was reluctant to take on the new job, claiming that architecture was not his strongest talent, but he was forced by the pope's insistence to accept it. He worked on St. Peter's until shortly before his death, and his appointment was confirmed by the next four popes who reigned after Pope Paul III's death, Julius III, Marcellus II, Paul IV and Pius IV.

Michelangelo had a very poor opinion of the work of his predecessor, Sangallo, and abandoned his form of a Latin cross to return to Bramante's original design for the church in the form of a Greek cross. This plan was modified after Michelangelo's death, when between 1607 and 1614, Carlo Maderno added a long nave to the church. Much of Michelangelo's other work on St. Peter's has been hidden by further changes made in later centuries, but his most famous contribution to the church is still visible: this is the circular wall that supports the main dome. He also prepared designs for the dome itself, and a wooden model of Michelangelo's initial project has survived. The dome was completed in 1590 by Giacomo della Porta, who added some decoration to Michelangelo's basic design.

The Conversion of St. Paul (detail)

In the same period Michelangelo also worked on other architectural projects in Rome. These included designs for the completion of Sangallo's work on the Palazzo Farnese and for the Church of San Giovanni dei Fiorentini, the conversion of a part of the ancient Baths of Diocletian into the Church of Santa Maria degli Angeli and plans for the façade of the Porta Pia, one of the gates of the city.

Although he was kept busy supervising work on his numerous building projects in Rome, in private Michelangelo returned to sculpture, his preferred means of expression. He experimented with new versions of the *Pietà*, a sculptural group showing the dead Christ lying in His mother's arms, sometimes with other figures. These were works that Michelangelo carved for himself with no obligations to patrons. One of these sculptures was the *Pietà* that he started in 1553, with Nicodemus, the Virgin Mary and Mary Magdalen holding Jesus, and it was originally destined for Michelangelo's own tomb. He wanted this to be built in the Church of Santa Maria Maggiore in Rome, and the face of Nicodemus in the sculpture is widely believed to be a self-portrait. Michelangelo later changed his mind, indicating that he wished to be buried in Florence, and he sold the sculpture. It was still unfinished, after he had deliberately broken the left arm and leg of Christ, as Vasari tells us, "because it was full of flaws." It was kept for a while by Tiberio Calcagni, one of Michelangelo's assistants, who finished the figure of Mary Magdalen in an academic style.

As he grew older, Michelangelo lost many of his dearest friends. His close friend and confidant Vittoria Colonna, a widowed noblewoman to whom Michelangelo dedicated many poems, died in 1547. His brother Giovansimone died in 1548, followed by another brother, Gismondo, in 1555. The same year saw the death of Michelangelo's servant Francesco Amadori, who had helped him while painting the fresco of *The Last Judgment*. Michelangelo, increasingly weary of his earthly existence, wrote to his nephew, Lionardo: "This death is a sorry tribulation for me, and I would have liked to have died with him."

In September 1556, Michelangelo was forced to flee from Rome, which was under threat of invasion by the Spanish army. He traveled east and took refuge in the rural town of Spoleto, whose countryside was to make a deep impression on him. The stark and somber backgrounds of his paintings had paid scant attention to nature; however, when he returned to Rome, urgently summoned by the pope to resume his work, he surprisingly declared: "Only half of me is in Rome, because peace can be found only in the woods."

Michelangelo's last sculpture was the *Rondanini Pietà*, in which the figures of Christ and Mary merge into a single form. Daniele da Volterra, the artist ordered to cover the blasphemous obscenities of *The Last Judgment*, saw Michelangelo working on the sculpture only a few days before his death. On February 14, 1564, Michelangelo fell ill, but although he was suffering a high fever, he continued to walk the streets of Rome, telling his assistant Tiberio Calcagni that he was unable to rest. Four days later, on February 18, forced to his bed by a stroke, Michelangelo died, attended by a handful of intimate friends. Daniele da Volterra made a death mask of his former master, and used this to cast a bronze bust that is probably the most accurate portrait of Michelangelo that we now possess.

A solemn official funeral was held for Michelangelo in the Church of Santissimi Apostoli in Rome. Two days before his death, however, the great artist had once more declared his firm desire to be buried in Florence, and his nephew Lionardo stole his body and smuggled it out of Rome in a packing case. Michelangelo was buried a second time, on July 14, 1564, in the Church of Santa Croce in Florence, and his sepulcher, designed by Giorgio Vasari, is next to that of Dante, the poet that Michelangelo so greatly admired.

Michelangelo's career seems to have been one of constant frustration. None of his major architectural projects were finished in his lifetime. He was forced to abandon sculpture, his favorite means of expression, for painting. He frequently declared himself to be barely competent in the painting of frescoes, yet he is probably best remembered for the superb frescoes in the Sistine Chapel. He worked for decades on a tomb that was reduced from a grandiose vision to a meager group of three statues, and was often obliged by wars or by the whims or even the death of his patrons to move on to new commissions before existing ones had been completed. Nevertheless, his legacy is one that has influenced generation after generation of artists and architects, although probably Michelangelo would never have believed that this might be possible. Shortly before his death, he destroyed many of his drawings, and declared: "If I were to gain satisfaction from what I have done, then I would have done less, or perhaps nothing at all." And this sense of humility remained with Michelangelo to the end, as the words of his final confession reveal: "I am sorry that I have done too little for the salvation of my soul, and that I must die when I have just begun to learn the alphabet of my craft."

The Holy Family (Doni Tondo)

View of the vault before the last restoration (Sistine Chapel)

Deluge (Sistine Chapel ceiling)

The Fall and Expulsion (Sistine Chapel ceiling)

The Creation of Eve (Sistine Chapel ceiling)

The Creation of Adam (Sistine Chapel ceiling)

God Separating Earth from Water (Sistine Chapel ceiling)

The Creation of the Sun, Moon and Stars (Sistine Chapel ceiling)

Ignudi near *God Separating Earth from Water* and *The Persian Sybil*
(Sistine Chapel ceiling)

Ignudo (Sistine Chapel ceiling)

Delfic Sybil (Sistine Chapel ceiling)

Cuman Sybil (Sistine Chapel ceiling)

Libyan Sybil (Sistine Chapel ceiling)

Geremiah (Sistine Chapel ceiling)

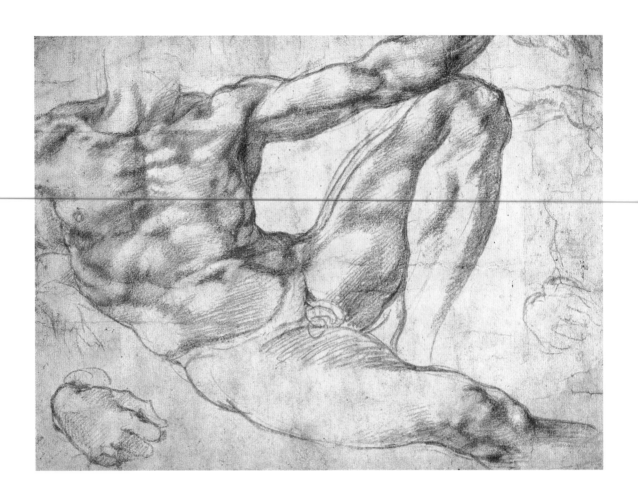

Study for *The Creation of Adam*

Study for *The Last Judgment*

View of the vault after the last restoration (Sistine Chapel)

The Last Judgment (Sistine Chapel)

Christ and the Virgin (*The Last Judgment* detail)

Angels and Archangels (*The Last Judgment* detail)

The Damned (*The Last Judgment* detail)

St. Bartholomew (*The Last Judgment* detail)

Crucifixion of St. Peter

Bacchus

Pietà

Pietà (detail)

David

Bruges Madonna

Pitti Tondo

Taddei Tondo

The Tomb of Pope Julius II

The Tomb of Pope Julius II (detail) *Moses*

Bearded Slave

The Young Slave

The Awakening Slave

The Slave (Atlas)

The Dying Slave

The Risen Christ

The Tomb of Lorenzo de' Medici

The Tomb of Lorenzo de' Medici (detail) *Lorenzo de' Medici*

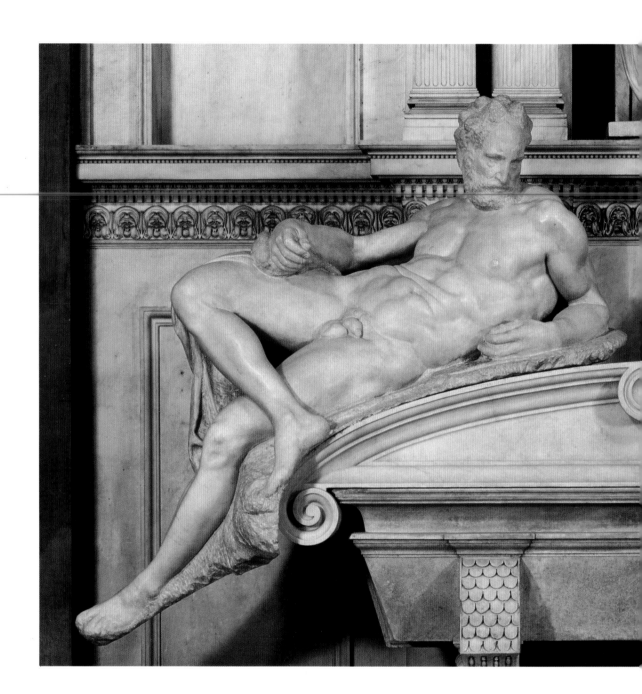

The Tomb of Lorenzo de' Medici (detail) *Twilight and Dawn*

The Tomb of Giuliano de' Medici

The Tomb of Giuliano de' Medici (detail) *Giuliano de' Medici*

The Tomb of Giuliano de' Medici (detail) *Day and Night*

The Victory

The Victory (detail)

Pietà